BINARY OPTIONS:

Steps by Steps Guide to Making Money from Binary Options Trading

by

Benjamin Daniel

LEGAL NOTICES

COPYRIGHT

All rights reserved. No part of this book may be reproduced in any form whatsoever, electronic or mechanical, including photocopying, recording, or by any informational storage or retrieval system or re-distributed without the express written permission of the author. This book cannot be sold under any circumstance; you have only personal rights to this book.

DISCLAIMER

By using the information in this book you agree that this is general education material and you will not hold anybody responsible for loss or damages resulting from the content provided here by the author

Please note that Binary trading and trading in other leveraged products involves a significant level of risk and is not suitable for all investors. Before undertaking any such transactions you should ensure that you fully understand the risks involved and seek independent advice if necessary. Any opinions, or other information contained in this book are provided for general educative purpose, and do not constitute investment advice.

Copyright © 2018 Benjamin Daniel

All rights reserved.

TABLE OF CONTENTS

LEGAL NOTICES 1
TABLE OF CONTENTS 2
INTRODUCTION 4
CHAPTER ONE 6
    WHAT IS BINARY OPTIONS? 6
    BENEFITS OF BINARY OPTIONS TRADING 7
    BINARY OPTIONS TYPES 8
CHAPTER TWO 10
    HOW TO TRADE BINARY OPTIONS 10
    UNDERSTANDING THE TREND 10
    WHAT IS TREND? 11
    UP TREND/BULLISH TREND 12
    MANUAL METHOD OF DETERMINING UPTREND 12
    ARTIFICIAL METHOD OF DETERMINING UPTREND 14
    DOWN/BEARISH TREND 18
    METHODS OF DTERMINING BEARISH TREND 18
    SIDEWAYS/RANGING 21
CHAPTER THREE 24
    BINARY OPTIONS TRADING SIGNALS 24
    BUY/CALL SIGNALS 24
    SELL/PUT SIGNALS 30
CHAPTER FOUR 34
    MONEY MANAGEMENT STRATEGY 34

    HOW TO USE MARTINGALE STRATEGY 35
CHAPTER FIVE 38
    CONCLUSION 38

INTRODUCTION

Thank you for laying your hand on this book. I strongly believe the ultimate purpose of you getting this book is to take part of the Binary Options cake. Believe me, this is surely reachable and attainable.

All you have to do is literally follow all the principle and strategy outlined in this book and you will be guaranteed to **CONSISTENTLY** have high winning ratio which translates to a very striking Return on Investment (ROI).

Please note this is not a get-rich-soon scheme. It requires some level of self-esteem and disciplined on your part.

You don't need to have any prior knowledge of Binary Options or Forex Trading; though this would be a plus… Though if you have prior knowledge, it will be an advantage, but notwithstanding I will take you by the hand in this book and show you step by step how you can trade profitably even if you don't know anything about Binary Options before.

In this book, all you need to succeed in this business have been greatly outlined. The only skills you need to start your path of wealth growth are

- Discipline – Follow exactly the steps in this book
- The Will to implement what you learn or taking action based on what you've learnt
- Binary Options account and;
- MT4 platform

I have great confidence that what you will learn, if implement will grant you consistent profit from Binary Options Trading.

CHAPTER ONE

WHAT IS BINARY OPTIONS?

Binary Options Trading is as easy as predicting if a flip coin is up or down. Of course this is equally dangerous and will lean towards gambling if you don't possess the proper knowledge and tools allowing you to get the odds in your favour.

Binary Options also known as Digital Options are not new financial instruments, but thanks to the new technologies, these are now available to the public and present an easier and faster way to make money.

Binary Options are types of options where the payouts is made based on "all or nothing" contracts. Meaning, if you win then you'll win all amount of money that you were promised to have. On the other hand, if you lose then you'll lose all contract's value. In both cases, the win-loss is measured in cash.

Digital Options are either in an "On" state indication which means you are in the money or in an "Off" state implying you are out of the money.

The basic version of trading binary options is predicting price value within a specific period of time which is called the "expiration date" or the trade's "expiration time."

The value of the payout is determined at the onset of the contract and does not depend on the magnitude by which the price of the underlying asset moves so whether you are in the money by $0.01 or $0.03, the payout that you receive will be the same.

Binary Options are sometimes called all-or-nothing trades, meaning that either you are In-the Money (ITM) and you get the specified payout or you are Out-of-the Money (OTM) and you lose your traded amount.

Binary Options trading are a fast and exciting way to trade the financial markets. The payout rate is high compare to any other traditional financial trading.

For example, if a trader wants to trade EURUSD and buys $50 contract of Call Binary Options that has a payout rate of 70%. At the moment EURUSD is trading at 1.2071 points by 2pm when the trade was executed with an expiration of 30mins.

If by 2:30pm the price of EURUSD moved up by 10points (1.2081), it means the trader was right. In this case, the trader will gain 70% return on his investment. So with the contract amount of $50, the trader will get $35 profit. $85 will be returned back to his account. In this case, he is in the money.

But if the price of EURUSD fell and got to 1.9970 by 2:30pm that day, his prediction was wrong. He is out of the money. He will lose $50 he invested.

No stop loss, no targets, no complicated money management calculations. That's why it's a lot easier than usual/common trading. **With Binary Options you need to focus on two elements only: price direction and expiration time.**

Most systems only focus on price direction and forget the expiration time period which works as a time based stop loss. If your predicted price move correctly and failed to calculate the time-range of price action then you would still lose the trade!

BENEFITS OF BINARY OPTIONS TRADING

One of the main advantage of trading Binary Options is that the trader's risk is limited to the premium that the trader pays for a contract. In the above example, the risk taken by the trader is limited to $50 in that particular position. This gives the binary options trader a feel of security in knowing that their downside is only limited to the initial trade size. While they can still profit if their market view turns out to be correct, they avoid having worry about stop loss order slippage or losing their trading discipline.

Besides, binary options offers a limited risk profile since they either pay off a fixed amount or they do not, depending on where the underlying instrument is trading at the expiration.

Another advantage is that it can be traded for shorter timeframes (5mins, 10mins, 20mins, 30mins etc) via trading platforms that offered such options. And this offers a great way to make more money within a short period of time than in Forex trading.

Also, it is very easy and faster to learn how to trade Binary Options than Forex or Futures trading. You will need to understand a lot of things to be able to trade Forex or Futures profitably but not so with Binary Options Trading.

BINARY OPTIONS TYPES

Several types of Binary Options can now be traded online using a variety of binary options trading strategies.

High/Low: The most commonly available binary options are high/Low also known as "Above" and "Below" or Call/Put binary options. You will receive a payout on High/Above/Call Options if the market price is higher than the entry price at expiration. When the market price is lower than the entry price at expiration, it is a Low/Below/Put options.

Some brokers offer one or more of these types of options like **Touch, Range or Boundary, Rise and Fall, Touch Not** etc.

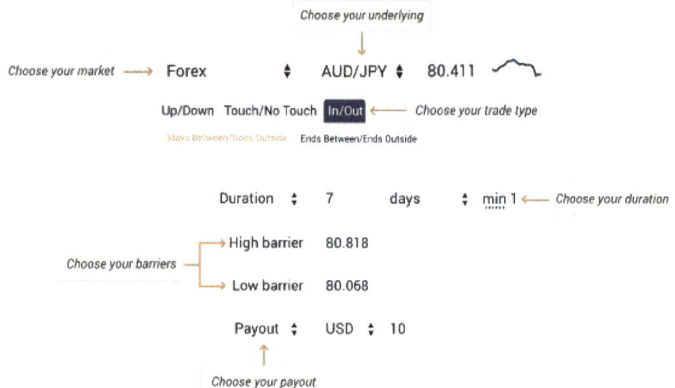

All markets: currencies, stocks, indices, and commodities.

All market conditions: up/down, touch/no-touch, stays between/goes outside.

All durations: from 10 seconds to 365 days.

All payouts: from $1 to $50,000.

CHAPTER TWO

HOW TO TRADE BINARY OPTIONS

Apart from having a good reliable broker to trade with, the first thing you need to understand before you can trade Binary Options profitably is a good strategies that gives you an edge to trade with the trend. In other word, you need a good understanding of the Trend and how you can trade with it, irrespective of the strategies you are making use of. This is the key to your success in this trade.

We are going to look at how to know the Trend and how to trade with it below.

UNDERSTANDING THE TREND

To really make money in trading be it Binary or Forex or Futures, there is no doubt about it, trading with the Trend is the only secret of making money. If you trade against the trend, you will lose. Trading with the Trend gives you 99.9% probability of turning the odd in your favour and making money from the Financial Market.

Now, the problem is how do we know the trend? What is the trend? How can we accurately know and depict the trend of the market without trial and error? If we can answer this question correctly, then it will be very easy for us to make money from the financial market.

WHAT IS TREND?

In a simple lay man's language, trend is the direction price of an instrument is going. If you are going to New York from Florida, the direction is like moving from the South where Florida is to the North where New York is. Your direction is going up.

Trend majorly is the direction of the market. Where is the market going? It is up or down or the price of the instrument is not even moving at all.

This is the very first question we need to answer any time we open the chart to trade. Once we can pick this very well, we will have no problem taking our trade.

And once you know the trend, then you trade alongside the trade. That is, you place your trade in the direction of where the price of the market is going. This helps you to follow the big boys where they are heading to, and you will surely make money.

Trend can be define in three ways.

   i.   Up Trend
   ii. Down Trend
   iii. Side Way or Ranging or Consolidation

There are two ways to pick or detect the trend.

   i.   Manual and;
   ii. Artificial or Using Indicator

I will discuss both ways in this book. We are going to discuss manual method first.

UP TREND/BULLISH TREND

MANUAL METHOD OF DETERMINING UPTREND

Up Trend is also refer to as Bullish Trend. In a Bullish or Up Trend, what we determine if the price is truly in an up trend is when price is moving up and it's having series of higher highs and higher lows.

That means in an Up Trend, price will move from a low to a high and pull back again to a new low which is higher than the previous low and shoot up to a new high which is higher than the previous high.

In an up trend we will have this pattern form on the chart. Low, High, Higher Low, Higher High. From L-H-HL-HH. That is the 1-2-3-4 pattern you will spot on the chart to know quite very well that truly the instrument is in up trend mode.

Now, let's see example in the GBPCHF Chart below,

We can see that price starts from Low move up to the High region and pull back to Higher Low and shoot up to Higher High and continue to form series of Higher high and Higher Lows. This is an Up Trend in action.

In this scenario, we are not going to place a sell trade. We will only look for opportunity to join the Up trend around each of the Lows. That is where we pick our buy trade. At the bullish Lows not the Highs. Please take note.

Let's look at another example in the chart below

AUDUSD Chart

Now, having gotten the true picture of what to look for in an Up Trend. Let's look at how we can use indicators to equally detect and know the direction of the Trend.

ARTIFICIAL METHOD OF DETERMINING UPTREND

In this method we are going to use Moving Average Indicator as a tool to help us. As we all know, Moving Average is Trend detector Indicator.

For our purpose, we are going to use Exponential Moving Average 8 & 21 and Simple Moving Average 20. We are using Simple Moving Average 20 (SMA 20) because is equally the Middle Band of the Bollinger Band Indicator. This is a very powerful Indicator that most traders take cognizance of in their trading.

Let me say this also, that Moving Average are serves two purposes.

1. To Pick the Trend and;
2. To determine the Key Levels on the Chart

Now, the key Levels are the various Resistance and Support Levels on the Chart. So we can use Moving Average also to create the Resistance and Support Level zones on the chart while trading.

When Price is moving up, i.e is in an Up Trend, Moving Average above the price or candles can resist the movement to the Up side and vice versa.

Now, get to your chart and insert EMA 8& 21 of closing price and SMA 20 of closing price as well.

See example below,

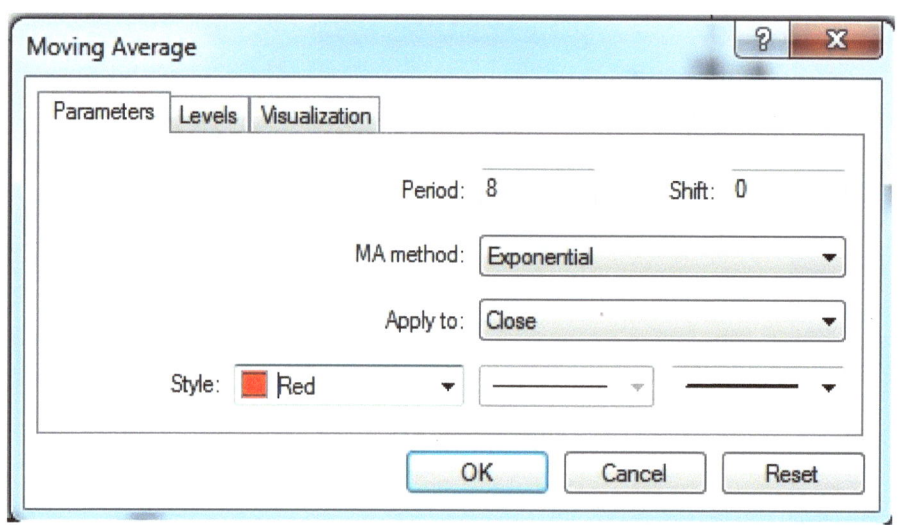

Once we have inserted them to our chart, how do we make use of it?

Now, this is what you will do.

Anytime the Candles Cross and Close Above the three Moving Average lines (EMA 8& 21 and SMA 20) then the Trend has changed to Up Trend. Please note, the Trend is really confirm only when the Candles close above the SMA 20. If candles are yet to close above it, we will disregard it. The trend is not yet confirm yet.

Again, **the Candles must crossed and close above the three Moving Average lines for the trend to be confirmed.**

And **in an Up Trend, the candles must continue to stay above the Moving Average lines for an Up Trend to be in place.**

So in an Up Trend, the candles will always stay above the Moving Average lines to the up side.

Let's see example below on the same chart we used above.

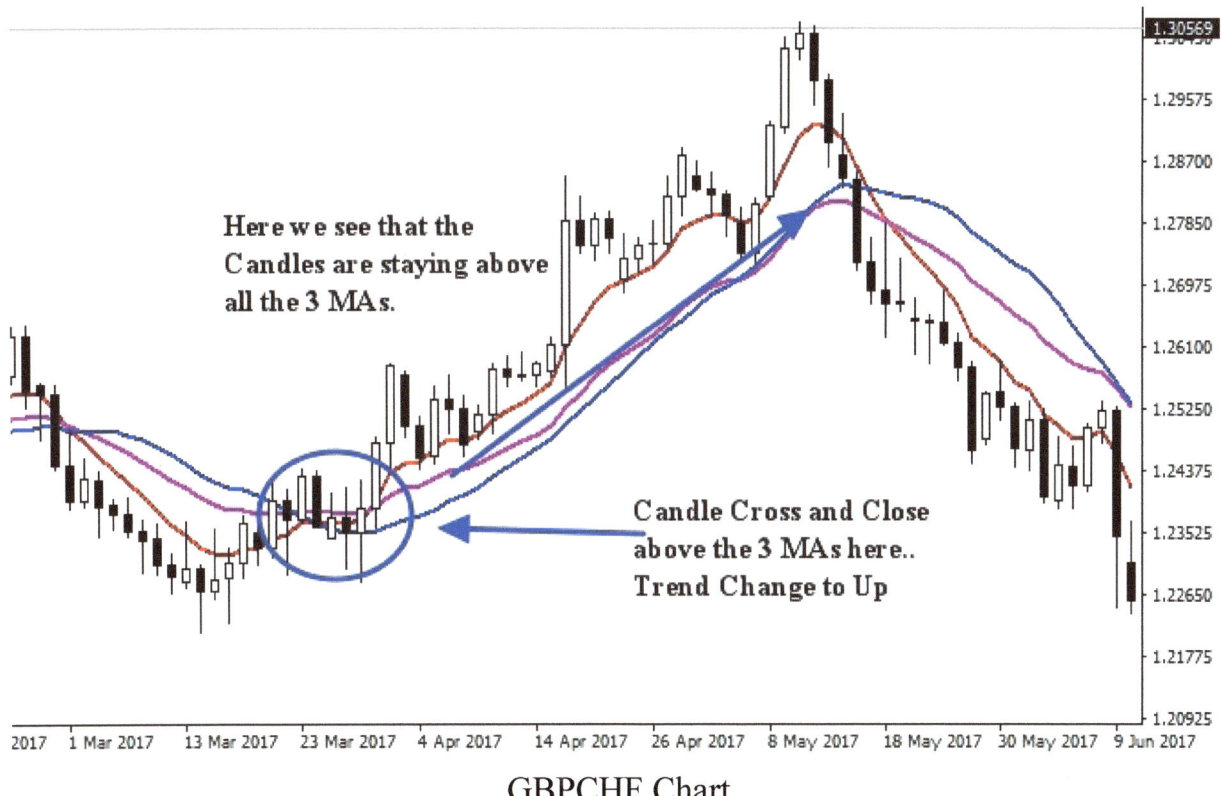

GBPCHF Chart

According to the Rule, we can see that in the circle above, the candle cross and closed above the three Moving Average lines, which indicate that the Trend has changed from Bearish to Bullish Trend.

Also, we can see that while the candles are moving upward, they are all staying above the three Moving Average lines. It must never be below the Moving Average if it is an Up Trend. Anytime it cross and stay below the Moving Average, we have the Bearish trend in place and not Bullish Trend.

Let's look at the second chart we use above for this same illustration.

AUDUSD Chart

Now, let's move to the second item which is the Down Trend of Bearish Trend.

DOWN/BEARISH TREND

We determine a down trend when price keep making series of Lower Highs and Lower Lows. Remember when the price continues to make Lower Highs and Lower Lows, the trend is down.

So in other word, it will form this pattern High, Low, Lower High, Lower Low, Lower High and Lower Low in that order. Once we can spot this pattern on the chart, then we know a bearish trend is in place.

METHODS OF DTERMINING BEARISH TREND

Manually, let's look at how it looks like on the Chart.

The chart below is an example of series of Lower Highs and Lower Lows as we can see on a typical chart of USDJPY.

Now, let's look at what it looks like if we add indicators to help us pick what the trend is.

We can see in the chart above that the candles all closed and stayed below all the three Moving Average lines.

Though we have instances where the Candles revert back or pull back towards the Moving Average line, in each instances, we can see that the Trend continue as the

19

candles close below the Moving Average line and move downward strongly after each pull back.

Like we said, we also see that the Moving Average lines serves as Resistance inhibiting or resisting the upward move of the candles.
Let's look at another example for more clarity.

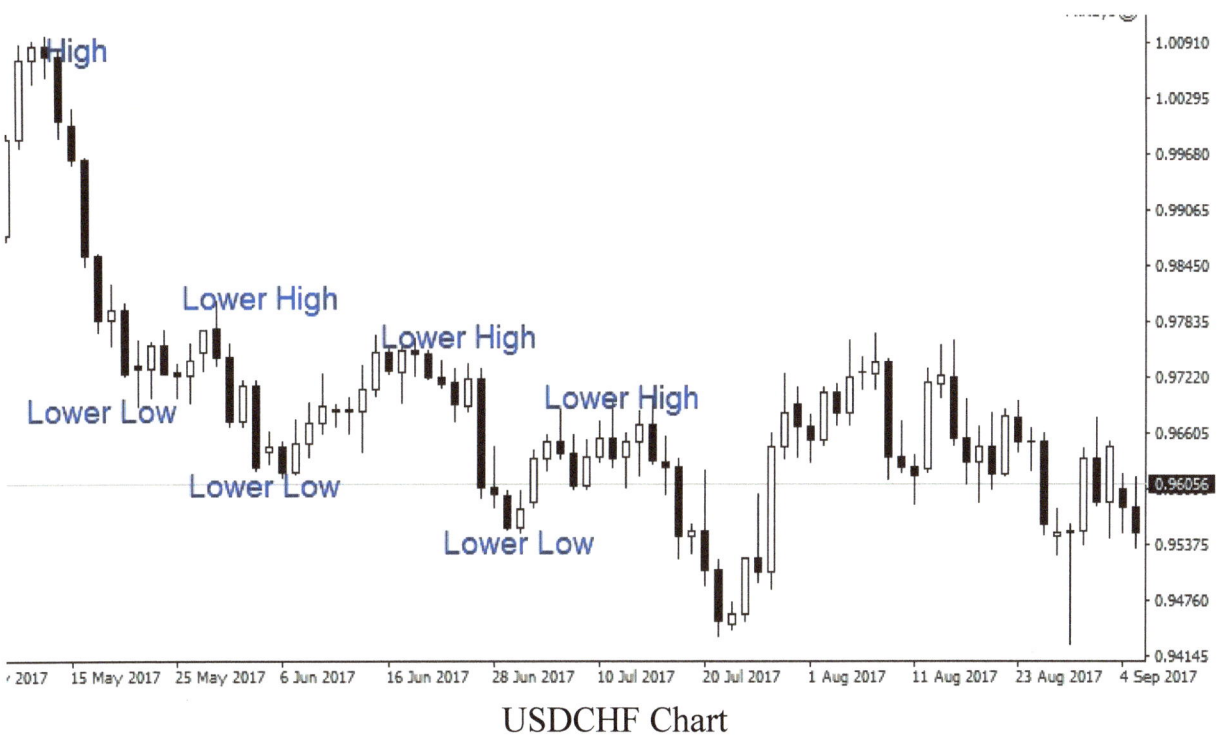

USDCHF Chart

USDCHF Chart

SIDEWAYS/RANGING

When price is neither moving up nor moving down but seem to be contained within a price range. Such a market is ranging. It can also be referred to as a consolidating market.

Let's take a look at USDJPY chart for instance,

Here in this chart, we can see that from February, 2015 to May, 2015 the price was lock in between 120.800 and 118.300.

Here the price is neither moving up nor moving down. It was ranging in between.

So for binary trading, we do not consider ranging market. Our Trading signals will be taken into consideration when the price is either in the UP Trend or Down Trend.

CHAPTER THREE

BINARY OPTIONS TRADING SIGNALS

Now, having understood what it takes for the price of an instrument to be a trending pair. Our next major step is to utilize this understanding to trade Binary. Now, like I have said, we are not taking consideration of ranging market condition.

BUY/CALL SIGNALS

There are two ways to take this signal.
   i. Aggressive and;
   ii. Conservative Way

I will discuss both ways and use chart to illustrate.

Rule 1:
(i) **When Candle cross and close above all the three Moving Averages. Place a trade.**
(ii) **In an Up Trend, Candle will be above the Moving Average. When the Candles run off or divert away from the EMA 8 and pull back in a corrective mode and close above any of the Moving Average with a bullish candle, place your trade.**

The first one is the Aggressive Way while the second one is the Conservative way.

Time Frame: 5mins and 15mins

Expiry: 5mins or 15mins

Let's see how this work out with a chart. In this chart. EMA 8 is in Red Colour, EMA 21 is the Purple line while SMA 20 is the Blue line.

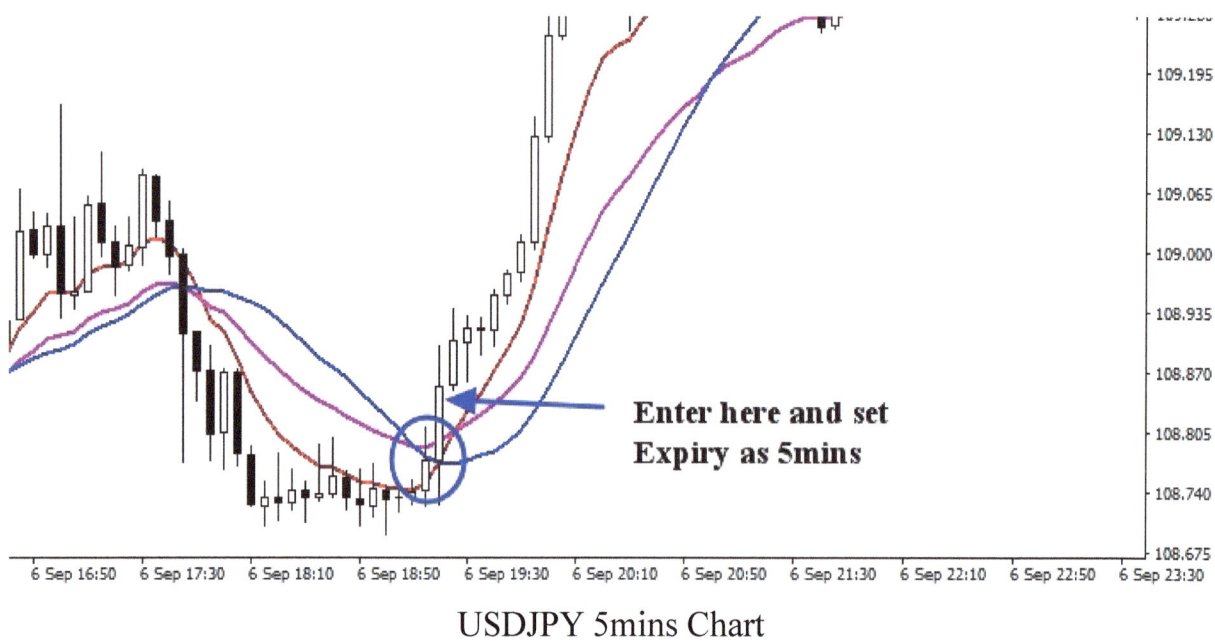

USDJPY 5mins Chart

Entry immediately after the cross above the three Moving Average is how to enter the aggressive way.

Let's look at another aggressive way of trading.

25

GBPUSD 5mins Chart

Please note that if the candle has not closed above the SMA 20, we will not regard the trend to have been changed.

Let's look at the Conservative way of trading which is safer. In this style, we will wait to confirm if the trend is actually what it says it is. Once we spot the Bullish Trend by the breaking of the Moving Average lines, then we wait for a pull back towards the Moving Averages lines, and as soon as we find another bullish candle formed, it indicates that the Bullish Trend is about to resume and we can then join the Trend.

Let's look at examples below,

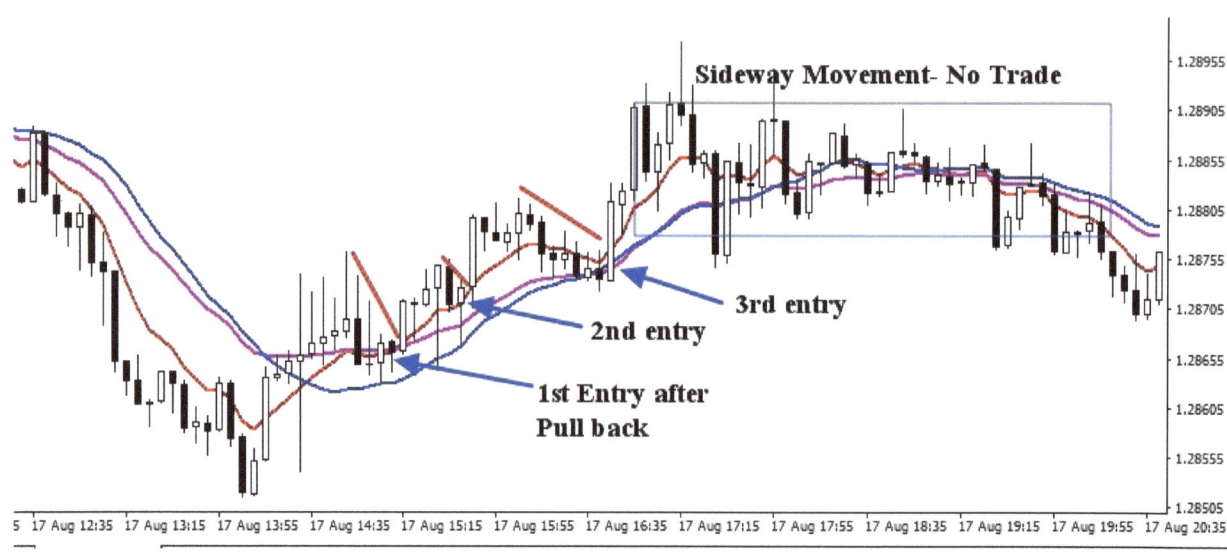

GBPUSD 5mins Chart

In the chart above, I have denote the Pull back or retracement using the Red Line. I hope you can see it on the chart.

Now, in the above example.

The first blue arrow shows the Bullish Candle that close above the Moving Average after the retracement has ended.

Once you find this set up. You place your trade for the next 5mins. (Expiry is 5mins)

Now, it is very possible that the price might not take off immediately. If you observed the chart above, you will see that the next candle after that bullish candle was bearish which means if you have entered that trade, it will be a loss.

So what you will do is you enter another trade using Martingale Strategy. You will double your stake so that the first loss will be recovered and the new second trade you will get profit out of it.

The reason why we will not change the direction is because we are trading in line with the trend.

The summary is as below,

Entry: Bullish close after the pullback.
Expiry: 5mins
Money Management:
1st Trial (Stake): $5
2nd Trial (Stake): $10
3rd Trial (Stake): $20

If after the 3rd attempt it is still a loss, then you may need to leave it and find another good set up.

Let's look at another example

USDCAD 5mins Chart

The Candle in the circle is the start of the Trend. Then we wait for a pull back. The pullback was confirmed by the first entry as indicated by the arrow.

Place your trade and set your expiry as 5mins.

Another attempt was indicated by the 2nd and 3rd arrow.

Let me show another example

This is 5mins chart of AUDUSD.

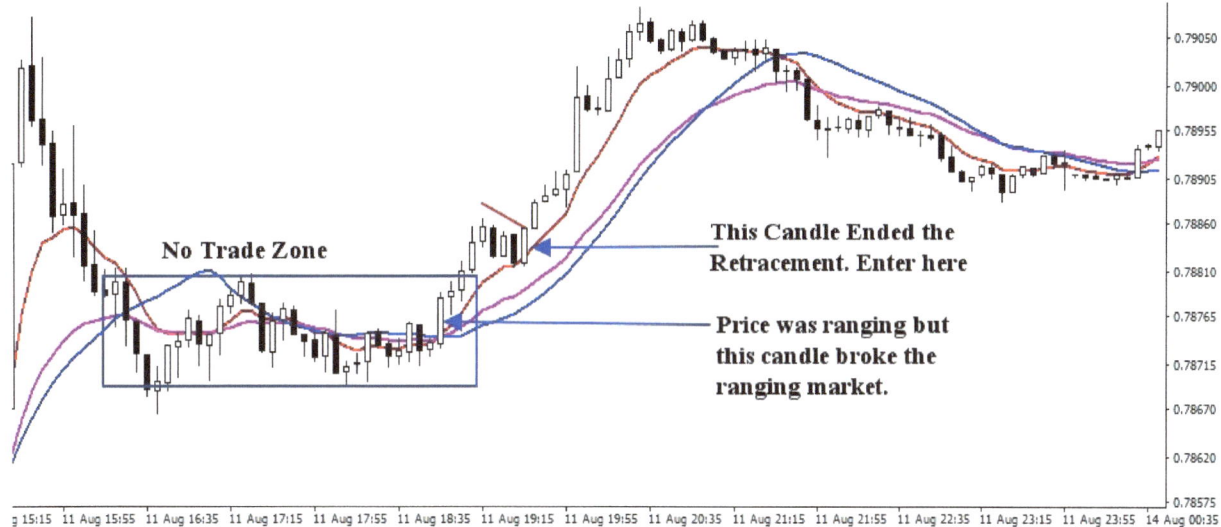

AUDUSD 5mins

Please note that there is no trading system that is 100% perfect. The best thing is to look for the best set up and trade.

We have more than 26 pairs in the Forex market. If you open one chart and it does not give you what you desire, then you can open another one until you find the best set up that will guaranty you profit.

SELL/PUT SIGNALS

The rules below are what to look for to place your Sell or Put Trade.

Rule 2:
   i. **When Candle CROSS and close BELOW all the three Moving Averages. Place a trade. (Aggressive)**
   ii. **In a DOWN Trend, Candle will be BELOW all the Moving Average. When the Candles run off or divert away from the EMA 8 and pull back in**

a corrective mode and close BELOW any of the Moving Average with a BEARISH candle, place your trade. (Conservative)

We are going to illustrate this ideal trade set up with examples for proper understanding.

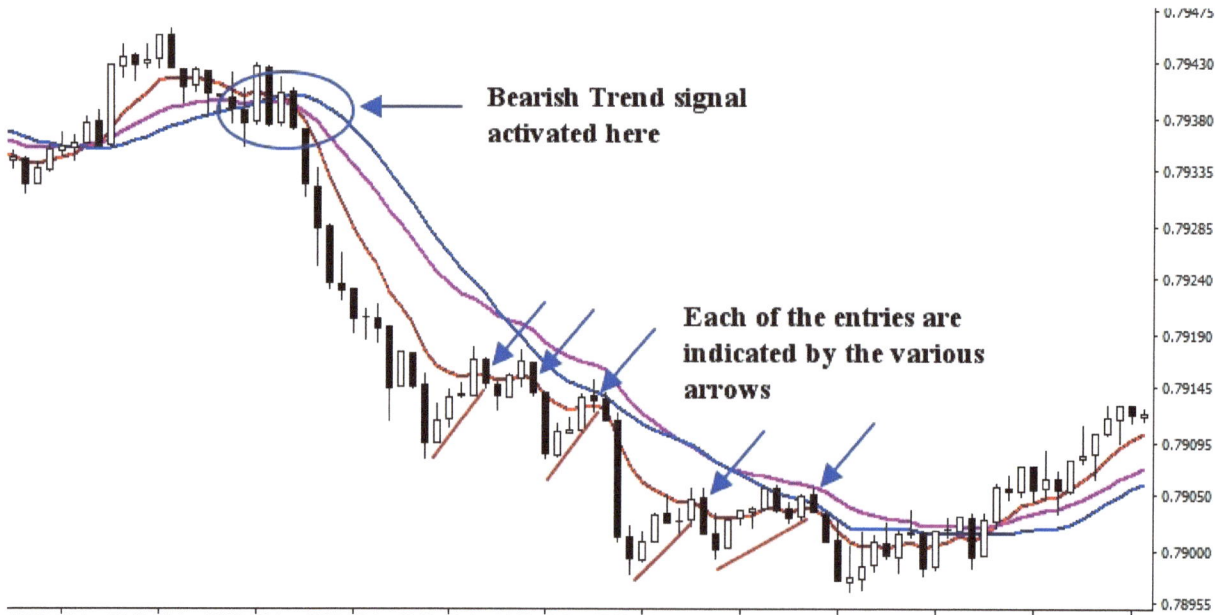

AUDUSD 5mins Chart

I have indicated pullback or retracement by the Red Colour line… hope you can spot it on the chart. The Pullback or retracement ended by the bearish candle as indicated by the blue arrow.

If you place your trade immediately after each of those bearish candle for the next 5mins, you will always win your trade.

Even if it doesn't win, you can place another sell or put for another 5mins with double of your stake and you are guaranty of success because you are trading in line with the Trend.

Let me show you another example,

The chart below is EURUSD 5mins

EURUSD 5mins

CHAPTER FOUR

MONEY MANAGEMENT STRATEGY

A good money management strategy is the key to successful trading business. Even if your strategy grants you 40% success rate, if you have a very good money management strategy, you will always end up in the winning side at the end of the day.

The edge we are trading with is the Trend. And as long as we have the Trend on our side, we will always profit.

This section aim at teaching you how to manage your money in such a way that you will have a plan and trade your plan.

Having a trading plan is one of the first step to effective money management strategy. Then you must have the discipline to trade your plan.

The trading signal described above gives a very high winning ratio because you are trading alongside the trend. However, without a proper money management, you risk depleting all your hard earned money.

The set of rules below are designed to make it easy for you to implement.

- Decide your Initial Investment Amount (Capital)
- Decide your risk amount: your minimum trade size

- Fix your minimum risk amount to 1% of your Capital. If you have a capital of $1000, in this case it will be $10. So it means for every trade, you are risking $10.
- For every trading day, start with your minimum risk amount of 1% ($10 in our example) and not your present balance.
- Place your trade only when your signal is confirmed.
- Make sure there is no news release when trading and that price is not near support / Resistance zone.
- If the result is a loss, then double your trade size in your next trade using Martingale Money Management strategy as shown below
- Above all, look for ten (10) good trade setup per day.

HOW TO USE MARTINGALE STRATEGY

Martingale is the best strategy to use to recover losses and still profit at the end of the day.

Please see the chart below for example,

80% Payout			
POSITION	SUM	GROSS PROFIT	NET PROFIT
1 €	1 €	1.80 €	0.80 €
2.5 €	3.5 €	4.50 €	1.00 €
6.25 €	9.75 €	11.25 €	1.50 €
15.63 €	25.38 €	28.13 €	2.75 €
39.07 €	64.45 €	70.33 €	5.88 €
97.66 €	162.11 €	175.79 €	13.68 €

The chart above is done with the assumption that you are having 80% payout. But it will be good to do a manual one that will be tailored to the payout of the market you are trading so that by the time you place your trade, the losses will be recovered and you will still be in profit.

For example, in the chart above, you start with an investment of $1 if you lose, you increase your stake to $2.5, if you lose, increase your stake to $6.25 in that order as seen above.

In each cases, you will recover your previous stake and still be in profit.

But I am very sure you won't lose consequently like this if you are trading in line with the Trend and you do the right thing. Please note that you can modify this Martingale strategy depending on your capital.

The strategy trades in line with the trend. It is expected that within the third trial, you would have recover your stakes and be in profit since we are trading alongside the trend. Anytime you win, start all over again with the initial stake.

Lastly, not all trades are wins. Do not be fearful and emotional and place trades. Stick to those set of rules exactly and you're guaranteed to have a consistent returns on investment.

The strategy works and have at least 70% success rate.

Willpower and discipline are two things that will help you to be a successful trader. To be a successful trader, you must sit down and trade based on your plan. A trading plan will make sure that you are following a trading method.

Implementing your strict money management rules and following them every day is a great key to success. Traders must be disciplined, stay in control and not let either fear or greed rule them. They must cut losses short, maximize gains and most importantly of all, protect their capital.

CHAPTER FIVE

CONCLUSION

Binary Trading is very easy to trade. However it requires a great deal of patience and discipline. Patience to wait for the signal and discipline to trade your plan. If you fail to trade your plan, you are planning to fail.

Use the above money management strategy or you create your own. Stay with it and wait for the signals to show up.

However you have to note that there is no trading system that is 100% perfect. If you have a system that grants you 60-80% success rate, your winning rate will be fine when you combine it with Martingale Strategy.

However, if you lose consistently it is good for you to quit the market for that day.

You must leave your emotions out of your trading. Trying to revenge back on the market to recover your losses will make you lose more. You have to know that the best trading decisions are taking when your mind is calm and cool to make decision.

I have strong confidence that trading with the trend is a sure bet any time any day in trading be it Binary Options, Forex, Futures or Stocks Market. And this book has done justice to place in your hand a strategy that will help you to trade with the trend and make you rich in Binary Options.

I do hope that not only reading this to gather knowledge is not what will put the money in your bank account, it is taking action. Practice what you have learnt and you will see the money roll in.

Wish you success in your trading.

****

Thanks for reading! If you enjoyed this book or found it useful I'd be very grateful if you'd post a short review on Amazon. Your support really does make a difference and I read all the reviews personally so I can get your feedback and make this book even better.

"Thanks again for your support!"

www.ingramcontent.com/pod-product-compliance
Lightning Source LLC
Chambersburg PA
CBHW040425220526
45473CB00004B/1346